Be Better, Not Bitter... It's a MINDSET!

Deforis Bonner-Dolford
Be Better, Not Bitter... It's a MINDSET!

Published by BooxAi

ISBN: 978-965-578-037-6

Be Better, Not Bitter... It's a MINDSET!

Deforis Bonner-Dolford

Prologue

You can do better, whether you're young or old, if you put your mind to it. Everything is a mindset. If you tell yourself you can, then you will. No matter what obstacles, circumstances you face or the background you came from, it's all up to you. This is your journey. If you know God and pray, that's like putting the icing on the cake. So go be your best self. Go be great. Because that's what you are, it's inside of you!

My book title was inspired by a sermon I heard at my church (The Fountain of Praise in Houston, Tx.) that my first lady and co-pastor preached (Dr. Mia K. Wright) entitled, Don't be Bitter be Better. I started thinking about life and how we are raised differently from birth by parents who most times do the best they can, but it's a journey. We all have a story. Some good and some not so good, but as we get older, it's all up to us to be better. They say if life throws you lemons, make lemonade. Some of us do, but some of us choose to stay with the lemons until they turn sour. Then we start to blame others when we all have a choice. Life is a choice.

About Me

My name is Deforis Bonner-Dolford. I was born and raised in a small town called Brenham, Texas. It is known for Bluebell Ice Cream. I was raised by my grandparents, John and Deforis Holt, my namesake. My mother was 14 when she had me. She was a teenager, in high school and not married. She had gone to Dallas that summer to visit her aunt and, being unsupervised, got pregnant by an older guy in high school. I don't know my father because his parents didn't want his career and life messed up because he was close to graduating high school. So my mother came back home to Brenham and had me. My grandparents took care of me so my mother could go back to school and graduate. I struggled growing up because my mother wasn't around or in that role as a mother. I kinda felt abandoned, but my grandmother explained that she was young and really didn't know how to take care of me. I understood as time went on. Later I thank God for my grandparents and how they raised me. I grew up right along with my aunt and uncle in a loving, nurturing home. My grandmother didn't work, so she cooked daily. She helped us with homework. She watched us freely play outside and be children having fun. We went to church regularly and participated in a lot of school and church activities. We had rules. We knew what was expected of us. In my opinion, we were raised with manners, respect for others and honor. We were raised to accomplish things, give and help others, and to love and be yourself.

I am grateful for my rearing. It has made me who I am today.

I have been an educator for 36 years now. I graduated from Texas Southern University in Houston, Texas with my Bachelor's in Elementary Education. I then got my Masters in Counseling. I am married and have my own two children. What you learn or know you try to pass on to your children, so rearing does matter. Here is my story.

In the beginning

First, let me say it does no good to be hurt and angry forever. If you carry that around with you, it only hurts you, not the person you're angry with, believe me, I know. You have to pray and let it go. God will help you if you release all of that frustration, so you can grow and soar.

When you get old enough, stop and look at your life, write down things you want to do. Look at and appreciate what your parents have tried to help you accomplish. If you have parents that support you, learn to appreciate and thank them. If you have parents that are never around or are negative, learn that it's not you. Parents have a lot going on or it could be how they were raised. When you're young, you don't understand all of this. It's painful and you don't know where it's coming from, so you don't know how to process it. All we know as kids is what we see and hear, so from that, we feel a certain way. For example, if your parents are alcoholics and you see them drunk all the time, something is causing them to do this to themselves. As a child, you love them, so you try to help them. It hurts to see them this way. In return, you may get called names or hit. It's not you, it's the alcohol or what they are going through that causes this. You start feeling rejected, abandoned, and confused. As you get older, it's up to you to say, okay,

I've seen this my whole life and I don't want this. I can do better. Sometimes we choose what we see even though we don't like it. We feel we can't do better, but you can. It's a Mindset!

Another example is maybe your parents were abused when they were young and now they start slapping, beating or abusing you. Again, you don't know where it's coming from, but it hurts and you know it's not right. It's your parents' problem, but they need help first. You have to see this behavior isn't right and not continue the cycle. This is how generations of issues occur. We have to remember when we become a parent to not repeat the things we didn't like as children. I told myself I wasn't going to have a child in high school and I didn't. I told myself I was going to college and get a job and I did. I told myself I have to communicate in a relationship. I told myself I was going to get to know my mom, love and support her. I did just that. I enjoyed getting to know her after I got out of high school. I enjoyed being around my mom and going places with her.

Next phase

If you don't release all of that toxic negative energy, it weighs you down. You start making poor decisions, getting into trouble, have poor relationships with others and later, it affects your health because it's stressful. Again, who gets hurt? You do. It's not worth it. You may not even realize what you are doing. It's true that hurting people hurts other people. I know a lady whose daddy was killed when she was only four years old. She was a daddy's girl. She was angry. She started getting into trouble at school. She started fighting. She was out of control. She left home at age 15 because her mom couldn't tell her anything. She started doing drugs, stealing, drinking, went to jail, was raped, had a baby at 16. She couldn't keep a relationship. She said she had no one to look up to since she had lost her dad. She hit rock bottom because her dad was gone. She was angry, hurting, and making bad decisions. Her dad would have been so hurt seeing her choices. The cycle repeated itself because at age four, her daughter didn't have a parent because she was locked up in prison.

When you do all of this to yourself, then try to get yourself together, you've messed up, so it's hard to recover. You can't find a job with a felony. You need assistance to get on your feet so you struggle. Yes, you can change and go on to be great, it's up to you what you do with your mindset and your opportunities. You hold you back. You get caught up, then want to blame others for your mistakes. You decided to drink, you decided to do drugs. You decided to go join a gang looking for love. You don't like asking for help. If you need help, go get help. That's why there are counselors, church advisors, therapists, psychologists, and psychiatrists.

It starts by looking at your life/self

Everybody has dreams and desires. Write your dreams down. Set goals for yourself and work toward them. I told myself all my life I wanted to be a teacher. I played teacher growing up. I loved helping my teachers. I had teachers in my family that I hung around. Whatever your passion is, get it in your spirit. Dream it, do it, see it, speak it and be it. If basketball is your thing then all you think about is playing ball. If modeling is your thing you practice those walks, you get in the mirror and play with your hair. If you want to preach you learn scriptures. You start helping others and serve at church. I had a student in class, all he did was draw in his free time. He was perfecting his craft. I told him you have a gift and one day you are going to be great. I had another student who could sing. I told her you keep practicing and start doing little things like being in a choir, or singing at talent shows or at church. I told her, "One day you will be a star." I had one student, all he did on the computer in class was watch baseball. He loved the game. He got a baseball scholarship to go to college. I was so proud because I knew he loved it. One of my favorite students had speech issues. She was so smart. I helped her get therapy. She had so much talent she could sing, act, and was wonderful at coming up with creative ideas. I encouraged her, "Do not let speech get in your way, you have too many gifts." One day I know she is going to be a big star doing something great. She has great parents too. That makes a world of difference. I had another student who loved to cook. I said, "Girl, get into culinary classes so you can be a top chef and open that world famous restaurant." Whatever you are interested in, you have to nurture that dream. Yes, you will have pitfalls, but if that's your heart's desire, don't give up on you or your dream.

My journey as a parent

When I had my own two kids I raised them how I was raised. Again, we normally do what we have learned, unless it was not right, then you need a mind shift. My husband had been raised totally different from how I was raised. So, ladies, that's when you have to communicate. This really needs to be done when you're dating before the kids come. Otherwise you may have some issues. Children and child rearing is one of the causes of divorce. This needs to be discussed before marriage. Some people don't want kids. You need to find out about the person's family life. You need to ask about how they were raised so you can discuss what you all will and want to do. Parenting styles are important. Having structure is important. Support, love, nurturing are important. Who will help and do what is important? I have always thought parenting needs to be shared. Kids need both parents. I can't teach a boy how to be a man. I'm not one. Kids need to know their parents even if the parents are not together. The only thing that shouldn't be shared is personal situations between the parents. I hate when parents put their issues on kids or use them, or make the child feel as if they have to choose. No, you did that. It's your issue, not the child's. Later, if the other person is not so great, let the child see that and form their own opinion. You don't point out their faults, because again there is a reason for that. Maybe that child can help get them on the right track. Love and support is a powerful and beautiful thing. We all need it.

You need to discuss strengths and weaknesses, how you were disciplined, what structure looked like in your family, how to support expectations, how to guide. Children need to be kids, but they must be taught things like manners, discipline, do's and don'ts in the house and away from home. They need to know what you expect in public, what you expect at school. They need to know you listen to them and care. You have to spend time with kids and not just buy them material things. I see parents that buy, buy, buy, and the kids aren't passing. The parents don't come to visit the school. You can't get them on the phone. When you do talk to them, they make excuses for the child. They don't discipline because they hardly see them. They don't know if the child has homework, if the child is passing. They are parents in name only. To me that's not being a parent. Don't get me wrong, I know parents have to work. I know nowadays homes are mostly single parent homes. I know parents have a life and need rest but remember your child. They are suffering from lack of attention. They are feeling abandoned, neglected and that's how trouble begins. Kids start trying to find love, get some attention. Most kids are not bad, they just need some time. As a parent they are your responsibility. You must teach them right from wrong. If you're not present, the streets or people who are doing wrong will. Remember, we do what we see and hear, we learn by example. We think it's right if no one guides or tells us differently. That's why I hate when people say kids are different now. Yes, technology is here and that's great. But we are not monitoring what they do, watch, or hear. We are not correcting the bad input so they think it's all good. We don't know their friends or the families they come from. We let them go wherever, we let them spend the night at their friends' houses. This is how it starts. We don't take the time to find out stuff, we just take their word. We just let them go. This is how rape happens. This is how teenage pregnancy starts. This is how some lose their lives, because we don't know what they are doing or who they are with. Kids will tell you anything. Stop and find out because you are the parent trying to raise your child right.

Stop with the excuses

P arents, who don't do what they need to do, make excuses for their child and that sets the child up for failure. First, they learn you will lie for them. They learn you will take up for them, so they learn they don't have to do certain things. Kids come to school with no homework, kids aren't passing, kids sleep in class and kids refuse to work at school. Why? Because they have been up all night watching tv. Parents don't ask about homework and you assume they are going to school and they are passing. Again, you haven't taken the time to ask or find out, so the child does what they want to. You don't set any expectations for them and will tell the teacher they do their work. They will do better. They know you don't ask or require it so they don't do it. Yet some parents will act out if the child fails, but it's partly your fault too. They are children and you have to know what they are doing. I wouldn't want my child passed on when you know they haven't learned anything. Life is hard enough without lowering their self esteem. They need to feel good about themselves. They need to at least know how to read and enough math to count money on a job or open a bank account. You need to remember, they will one day be on their own. You shouldn't want them at home forever. They need to be productive. You may disagree, but I don't advocate just passing kids on to the next grade if they haven't done the work. It hurts them later on in life. Kids need to learn. If nothing else, how to manage themselves and their time. I do believe every kid can learn. I know every kid has potential, some may struggle, but if they get help they can be successful. Some parents send kids to school just so the teacher can babysit. They don't want to be bothered. I say maybe those parents shouldn't have kids then. Kids will be kids and it takes a lot to raise a child. It takes time, love and patience. If you don't have those to give, don't have kids. Some people have a lot of kids and don't do anything with them. The kids are just on their own. The parent is doing them a disservice and the kids grow up lost.

The system

Not only are the parents not raising and doing right by the kids, the politics of the system is a mess. The system has failed the kids. I love teaching, but you can't teach anymore. All the rights belong to the parents and the kids. The kids don't want to do anything and the parents aren't going to make them. Yet we are responsible for test scores. In Elementary school this is their foundation and we work hard to get them to learn. Again, the parents don't bring them on time. They don't have what they need and the parents don't support us. The system wants you to pass them regardless of their grades. Parents want to say we aren't doing our job if they fail. So, they fall through the cracks, being pushed on when some are not ready. Some are immature and need time to grow. Some parents do support them when they are in elementary school, but after that, they slack up. They need parents even more in Jr. High and High School because that's when they need help with decisions. That's when peer pressure sets in. That's when they need your guidance. So don't be absent. Ask how was your day? How are your grades? Get them the extra help they need. If not, we lose them. A lot of suicide sets in at this stage, if we are not there for them. This is when they start slacking and you need to know it. When they get to High School they get real lazy, if you're not aware of it, they fail. Yes, they think they are grown then, but that's when their mistakes start to happen. Their grades slip, they run with the wrong people, they feel the need to be popular or they feel isolated like they don't fit in. This is when they start dealing with relationships and participating in things. This is when they start feeling like I'm not a girl or boy and have gender issues. So they need you as a parent. They start drinking and experimenting with drugs and sex. This is when they think about running away. This is when they don't know who they are or why they are feeling what they are feeling. If you're not there, they sometimes start getting into trouble that can affect the rest of their lives. The girls get pregnant or boys go to jail. They start going to detention at school. This is when rearing kicks in. This is where support is needed. This is a crucial time for self esteem. I do believe a mind is a terrible thing to waste. During this time is when, if not moni-tored, the mind is wasted. It's so easy to get off track so parents, please help your child during their Jr. High and High School years. Don't let them just come to school and eat and sleep in class. Don't let the gap in their learning get bigger. Don't just allow teachers to pass them or the system to fail them by promoting them when they aren't learning. Don't make excuses and fault the teachers. We are great. We all have potential and ability to be whatever we want to be but you have to put forth some effort. We all do. Yes, let them participate in sports or school activities that build pride, community awareness, and help them grow and develop but, even with this support, make sure they are learning and developing in class and life.

This generation

P eople say this generation is different, yes, they are, but not in terms of what they need, but in terms of parents being younger or raised differently. They have too many kids and a lot of different fathers and no one is really doing anything with the children because the parents are young and have their own lives. They don't realize having kids is a big responsibility. Children require a lot of time, support, nurturing, guidance, love, understanding and patience. If you're not willing to do or give this then you shouldn't have kids. Grandparents aren't like they used to be either. The grandparents are younger and don't want the responsibility either. The kids end up raising themselves or something, or someone else raises them. The streets, gangs, drugs, they start looking for love in all the wrong places. They will tell you, "I do what I want to. I don't have rules. My mother is never home. I'm by myself a lot." So whatever influences they are around, that's what or who they pattern themselves after. If a girl is wild and having sex, is your child's best friend, your child too will think that's cool. If the boy next door is selling dope and has money, your child too will think that's great. Kids think… If my friend is shooting up and feeling good, I too will try it. Why? Because my parents aren't around to guide me, help me, tell me that's wrong or show me differently. Then next I start thinking about how I can do stuff, get away with stuff or how I can make these things happen in my life. If my parents aren't around then I feel a certain way. I'm lonely, depressed, feel abandoned, rejected, unloved so I start doing me. I then start making the wrong decisions. Next thing you know, my life starts to spiral out of control. This then becomes my reality. I may be in trouble, I may be pregnant, I may have a disease, I may be addicted, I may be caught up in a gang. These are all situations that I may not be able to handle or get out of. I may be in an affair, raped or caught up. Why? I didn't have the guidance I needed. From there I start picking up bad habits, talking back, lying, stealing, drinking, or smoking. I'm doing a lot of bad things now, not knowing it's affecting my life. My attitudes and actions now are bad. Normally that's when people can't tell you anything. You say, "They don't know my life and won't help me." You get caught up and lose yourself. Behind your choices. Yes, the parents are partly to blame for not being there but once you get school age you should be able to see or feel that this ain't right. You should want better or more and choose to hang around better.

All of us have great potential and dreams but we all need help. We can't do it by ourselves. Parents, you must, even if you didn't have it, try to give your kids a chance and break that pattern. Be there for them. Teach them right from wrong. Get the help they need if you can't give it to them. Quit doing and saying anything in front of them, the cussing these days is out of control but that's what they hear at home. If you have a problem, don't put it off on them. If you have relationship issues, don't put them in the middle or use them. Yes, work to pay bills and feed them but spend time with them. Take them places and teach them how to act. Make them respect you and others. Quit buying them material things if their grades aren't good or just because someone else has it. They need you, not stuff. We buy stuff and kids don't want it or use it. So that's money wasted. We buy stuff and they misuse it or don't take care of it. Some parents don't know where their kids are when they get home and they don't care. They don't ask or try to find them.

They just go lay down or do whatever it is they do. These are your kids. But if they get hurt or killed we want to blame someone else. We have to own up to what we are doing. Do better, regroup, think, and start doing what's right and move on.

Scenarios

I know a student who had a baby and her parents supported her. She had to stop going to school, and she stayed home. The parents bought all the milk, diapers, and clothes for the baby. The girl never worked. She stayed at home and continued having babies. The parents didn't require her to work or stop having kids. Why? Because they babied the girl. They thought what she did was okay. That's how they raised her, so they had to take care of the girls' situations. She whined and complained she never got to do anything because of her kids. The parents let the daughter go out and have fun. What did she do? Come up pregnant again. The parents never taught her to be responsible. They took care of all her issues, because she didn't know how. They never took time to tell her or show her how to handle business, so she continued down this path of being dependent.

One student said she drank with her parents and did what she wanted. She talked back to her parents and said she would run away if they didn't let her do what she wanted. In high school, her boyfriend already lived with her. She fought with her parents and called the cops on them a lot, but she didn't work and had nowhere else to go due to her behavior. Now, you tell me, was she raised right? No, they gave up trying to discipline her, she ran them. No rules were ever established.

They gave her what she wanted and they had to continue or she acted out.

I know a boy that was in a gang. I asked if he was scared. He said no, they love me, help me and provide for me. They are my family. I asked what his parents thought about it. He said he raised himself. They were never there. He sold drugs, smoked weed, was already having sex. He had plenty of money and told me he was getting ready to buy a house and car at 16 and move out. I asked how he was going to do that. The guy he was selling drugs for was going to hook him up. He was like a father to him, he said. He provided the guns, the job, the money, the drugs and was getting him whatever he needed. He wasn't passing at school. He said he hated school, so I asked why come. He said, "My parents think I'm here so I come." He stayed in trouble at school. He said his parents didn't know or care. They aren't coming up here and if they do, I will lie to them and say I didn't do it or I'll do better because I know that's what they want to hear. He was angry with them and the world. He believed in his gun and drugs, though.

I know another student whose parents aren't together. They try to compensate for that with the child so they both give her and let her do what she wants to do. She is dating an older guy. The mom put her on pills so she is having sex. They know the boy mistreats her but say, "Oh, I can't get in it because she will be mad at me." You are the parent, not her friend. Guide her. Don't let stuff happen to her. The mom said she hates when the daughter won't talk to her. Stop trying to be the kids' friend and be her parent. First, you talk to your child and communicate about all the stuff you are letting her do. She has an older boyfriend. You let her get on pills of which you are saying she can have sex. Did you talk to her about all of this? Kids need to be talked to about situations. Communication is key. Life is hard, so we need to discuss things with them, if we are good parents, and allow them to know they are doing certain things we disagree with. If not, they won't learn about things or will get the wrong information from other places.

I have two students who live alone. The girl's mom works a lot and then stays with her boyfriend when she gets off. She leaves her money and food. She checks on her. The girl is angry and bitter. She curses a lot. She works and is constantly in trouble and deals with older men. I asked her why she was so angry and she said life sucks. I asked how she felt living alone and she hates it. She said I've had to grow up fast. I cook, wash clothes and pretty much do what I want to. That's why when teachers tell her to do stuff, she curses at them because she says she's a woman. I asked about her dad. She said he has a lot of kids and doesn't have time for me. Yes, she is struggling in school and sexually active with older men saying she wants attention and money for things.

The boy's parents work a lot. They have money. So he is left alone with money for food, a nice Porsche to drive and no one at home but him. He tries to please them because he wants to keep the car and money so he has the grades but he has friends that use him because he has these things. He befriends them because he's lonesome. He buys them food, gives them rides just to say he's hanging with people. They even spend the night with him because parents aren't at home. The friends brag that we eat good hanging with my friend because he buys us food.

I had another student who said her mom had so many kids she didn't care about her. She said her mom allowed her to smoke and drink with her. She said her mom fought and cursed a lot around her so at school the girl was a holy terror. She cursed the teachers a lot and stayed in trouble, so when mom did come to the school, yes, she wanted to fight the principal. What could you expect? The mom raised her like that. The student had a baby her last year in high school. Again the environment and influences of what she was around growing up. The apples don't fall too far from the tree. We are like our parents most of the time unless we make a choice later and choose to be different.

One student loved his mom. She loved to drink. He tried to help her but she would say things to hurt him. He just wanted some of her time. He got in trouble at school. They called her and she didn't go. She sent someone else up there. He got in trouble again and they called the law on him. He started doing big stuff to get her attention. She never gave it to him. He hurt himself trying to seek love and attention and is in prison. He tried to get it the wrong way by doing things that only hurt him. He was very smart and did a lot of good things but needed a parent. Again, hurting people hurts other people. The mom had issues and she couldn't see she was hurting him and hurting herself by drinking. She needed help and she needed to be able to help him and couldn't see it. He needed love and she couldn't see her past pain wasn't resolved. A lot of people end up in trouble or in prison seeking attention or doing things because they are hurting from a rearing issue or past hurt.

We have one student who was killed at a party. They were drinking and smoking but he was 16 out at 3:00 am. I asked why he was out so late. Did the parent know he was at this kind of party? The kids said he was dealing drugs. I said I thought he was a good kid. The kids said he did what he wanted to do because the parents provided the car for him and he had freedom. Please don't just buy for your kids. Again, I can't emphasize enough to know what your kids are doing, who their friends are, where they are going. Now they are without their son and wonder what happened.

Girls tell me they lie to their parents about who they are with and where they are going. I tell them that's dangerous in case something like this happens. They bring clothes to school and change to be like the friends they hang around. One friend had her stomach out so I bought a top and changed to wear my stomach out. I tell them to be yourself. You are not your friend. They say, "Oh, but my friend is cool and wears nice clothes." Again, I see the influence and ask or wonder, does this child get in trouble or are they leading them the right way?

One 9th grade student was dating a boy only at school, meaning she didn't date him out. He was controlling her, telling her what she could and couldn't do. I noticed that she was trying hard to do it. I said, "You are not being yourself and trying to please him." She said, "I know and I'm miserable. I don't have any friends, I can't eat with others or hardly talk to people without him having a problem with it. I only walk to class with him." I asked why, she said, "He doesn't want me talking to anyone but him." She cried during class. She said, "I can't take it anymore." She said she felt alone and didn't know what to do. I always ask kids if they talk to their parents. Of course, she said no. I asked why, she said, "She's always busy and told me I'm bothering her." Where is your dad? "I don't know." I love that the kids talk to me but nowadays you have to be careful with that because again students and parents will turn on you. Even though you want to try to help their child, the parents feel like you are in their business. They don't want you to know what is going on in their home. They feel like the child is okay and they are fine too. So even though I'm passionate about what I do, you have to pray and can only do so much.

Red flags

Life is a choice, so when you do stuff, don't blame others because there are signs and red flags that we ignore or don't want to see. We see them in all relationships, when looking for friends or a relationship. If they are yelling at you, putting you down, making you do stuff for them and you feel a certain way, but you think, well, they are your friend, no, that's a red flag. We feel our pain. You know when you don't like something, yet you choose to put up with it. It won't get better, it will only get worse. Anytime someone is putting you down you need to get away from that person. They will break your spirit and you lose your self esteem. I hear boys calling girls b...'s and they don't correct them but will answer them. Then the girls turn around and call each other that. I say no, you have a name, that's all you should answer to. Don't stay in mess, learn to love yourself and make new friends. Hurting people hurts others and they will continue if you allow it. This is how abuse starts. This is how you get used. Yes, you are getting attention, but at what cost? You are losing you. But when you are in low places, you feel this is okay because you don't know what to do or where to go. I see boys getting girls to bring them breakfast and they go with another girl. I see girls needing friends so the gay girls start kissing them, making them do stuff and telling them they are gay. I see boys angry about stuff who will hit girls or tell them to do what I say. They say, " Oh, I really like him because he has money, plays ball, or is popular and so on." I always ask, "What do your parents say about this? Do they know? How do you feel about getting treated like this?" Most say my parents don't know or they don't care. I feel ok because I want a boyfriend or girlfriend. Most parents don't know that their kids come to school and change clothes because their friend is dressed a certain way. Most parents don't know their child comes to school and doesn't do any homework. They eat and sleep in class. Most parents don't know their child is tardy in almost every class due to walking around with their friends kissing, etc. Parents aren't concerned about grades anymore. They don't care about homework, they just take their child's word. But if their child doesn't pass then it's your fault or the schools. You call parents and don't get any response. Or they lie to you, nothing ever happens or changes. Some kids do stuff to see if their parents will come or call. But they will say they are your responsibility from 7 to 3 so it's almost like don't call me. I even had one parent say, when I get home I feed him and he goes to bed. I knew she didn't want to be bothered. Don't get me wrong, this isn't all parents. In my years of teaching I had great parents. But I told my parents, we have to work together in order for your child to be successful. If they didn't want to work with me, I'd say please consider another teacher. In my classes we learned and worked every day. I thank God I didn't have many issues and had parents requesting me. They knew I cared. I needed them to care too. When I was teaching Elementary, all my students who did get in trouble later in high school either ran with the wrong people or had parents that never came to see me after numerous calls. I do believe it takes the village to raise the child. Children need structure and if you give it to them with love and they know you care, they will perform and do well. Some say what is **structure** to me: I say teaching them to respect people, having manners, and being responsible for taking care of things, not letting them talk back or do things without supervision. It's having set times for things or a routine. It's knowing the parents' expectation of what to do. **Support** is: how was your day, talking to them. Letting them know you care. Going to the school, calling the teacher, showing up for events, letting them talk to you about their feelings or whatever is happening with them. Eat a meal with them, take them somewhere, just be with them. To me, this is being a parent and being concerned about their rearing. Take care of the child's needs by providing food, clothes and shelter but also their emotional needs. **Remember, they represent you.**

A lot of kids are hurt and have abandonment issues, or feel rejected. The kids in foster care or these group homes are hurting. Kids are depressed and start having health issues or mental breakdowns because they are children and don't understand all of these situations that adults place them in because of their problems. Some parents place pressure and stress on their kids. Some allow them to grow up too quickly, putting them in danger or bad situations. To me this is what leads to dressing provocative, lying, stealing, cursing, rape, molestation, drugs, drinking, and trouble with the law, gun violence, suicide and shooting up places or people. Again, parents need to do better so the kids won't be bitter. If you're bitter or you know you have issues, go get help. Talk to someone, especially if you are getting ready to be a parent. Don't be selfish and hurt another person. Yes, tv, videos, rap music is all impressive, but guide that. You know they are listening to it so discuss the songs with them. Rappers usually rap about their life and environment so ask how they feel or how they relate to it. Kids see and hear a lot. Whether you know it or not, it does affect them. Kids love their parents, period. You are their parents, that's all they know. So you have to decide yes, I'm going to do right by them. Set some rules for your kids. **Stop trying to be their friend and be a parent**. Help them make good, wise decisions.

I had a student whose mother died and she had a breakdown. She was adopted but knew of her mom. She hadn't been told anything about her birth mom and the dad wasn't around either. The adopted parents assumed it didn't bother her since she wasn't living with her. She ended up having to get help because she had so many unresolved issues. They didn't tell her anything about the mom's situation but the child knew some stuff from other sources, but they didn't want to discuss anything with her because they said she didn't need to know and couldn't handle it. But if they weren't going to talk to her, at least ask if she was okay after hearing the news in reference to the mom's death.

Well rounded

Not all kids will go to college and that's ok. Just encourage them to be the best they can be. Help them learn a trade so they can be productive. Teach them to make their beds, show them how to cook something, even if it's just breakfast. They need to know how to wash clothes. Teach them morals and values even if you didn't get that from home. You have your own kids now so want more for them. Help them get a job. Teach them how to drive. If not, the world will make them go a different way. Every time I turn on the news I see another person robbing someone, shooting someone and that's someone's child. Where did the parents go wrong? It starts from birth and how you reared them. What have you shown or told them? What example have you set? If all you've tried to do is work to buy them $300 tennis but left them alone constantly, you failed them. If you left them with another person all the time and didn't do anything with them, you failed them. They need you. This will save them. So many kids in high school have sex, do drugs, drink and get pregnant because they don't have anyone there. Life is hard but when you have things that happen and you have no one to talk to or turn to, you hit rock bottom and start doing what you see or feel. Your influencers steer you wrong so you start to spiral down. Most of these kids could be helped or turned around if they had help. No one likes to fail. Kids don't like when they are feeling frustrated. They know when you care. They know when things feel right. They love it when you tell them they did a good job or reward them. They love when you come to school events and watch them perform. This builds pride and character. You're telling them they did right and it felt good.

Ladies, I'm sorry, if you know who their dad is you should let them see him if the father wants to. Don't put their father down, they will see it for themselves later if they aren't right. They need them and you need the help and vice versa. Don't make a difference among children. It's not the child's fault the relationship didn't work. They are still your child. Don't put them down or talk negatively to them. This breaks their spirit. It's hard recovering from that. Be positive with them. Pray for them and with them. Take them to church. Keep them active. If you don't have the money, the YMCA has reasonable activities, so does The Boys and Girls club. Promote their dreams and talents. Push and support them. If they can sing, get them in choir. If he or she is a good athlete, get them in sports. If he or she can draw, get them in art. If she talks a lot, get her in debate so maybe she can be your family's first attorney.

The help... finally

Do I believe things could be better? Yes, I do. I believe all kids have potential and can make it if they are guided, have structure, love and support. I believe it starts in the home. I believe if you need help, seek and get the help. I believe in God and the power of prayer. Knowledge is powerful. If you know better, you do better. I believe who we associate with makes a big difference in our attitude and behavior. I believe in change. I believe kids need us. I believe if we have issues, don't get into something new before you have healed and solved them. We all have baggage but it's how we handle the baggage that will determine how we proceed in life and in relationships. I believe communication is key. I believe life is beautiful, it's what you make it. I believe God gives us opportunities and it's up to us to create great choices. Life gets hard at times but we can make it. It's a mindset. Our beginning is based on how we were raised but we can decide to move forward with purpose. You don't have to stay where you are if you don't like it. Get out, get up and get moving to build the life you want. Life is important. What you decide to do is important. Your circle is important. Your choices are important so choose wisely. **THINK.** How will this help me? Am I learning from this? Don't keep struggling, putting burdens on yourself and others.

You can make it if you try. Don't keep doing the same things, getting the same results. Love you, don't keep putting yourself in the same situations. Do better so you won't be bitter. It's a mindset, it's all up to you. If you have kids or when you have kids, raise them right, do better. They have to live in this world and make decisions and be around others, so help them be the light in this dark world. The choice is yours to start today to make the change needed. If you're of age, start thinking about your life, reflect on your rearing or where you are now. Life can be great, it's a mindset. Be better, not bitter for you as a person. God bless you in your great life.